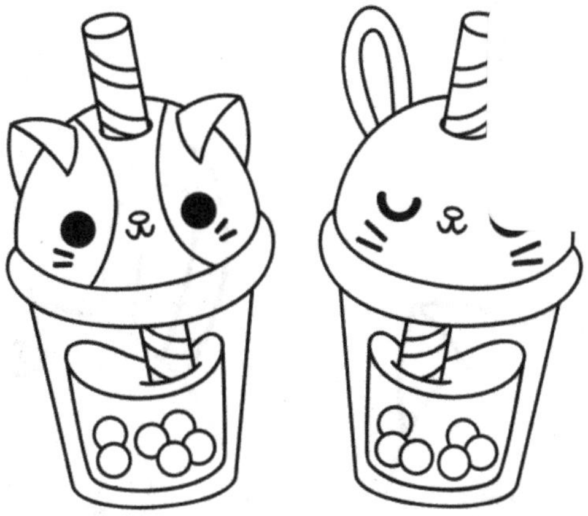

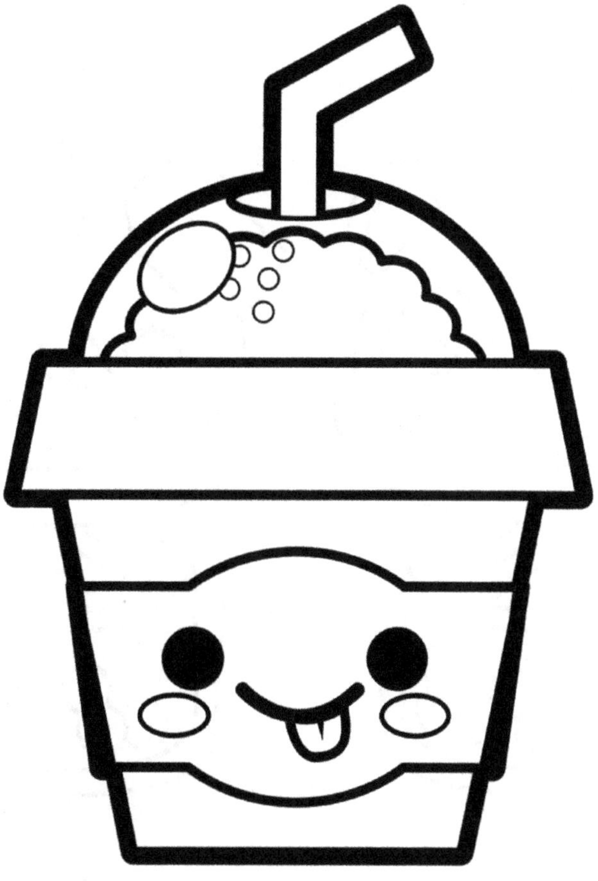

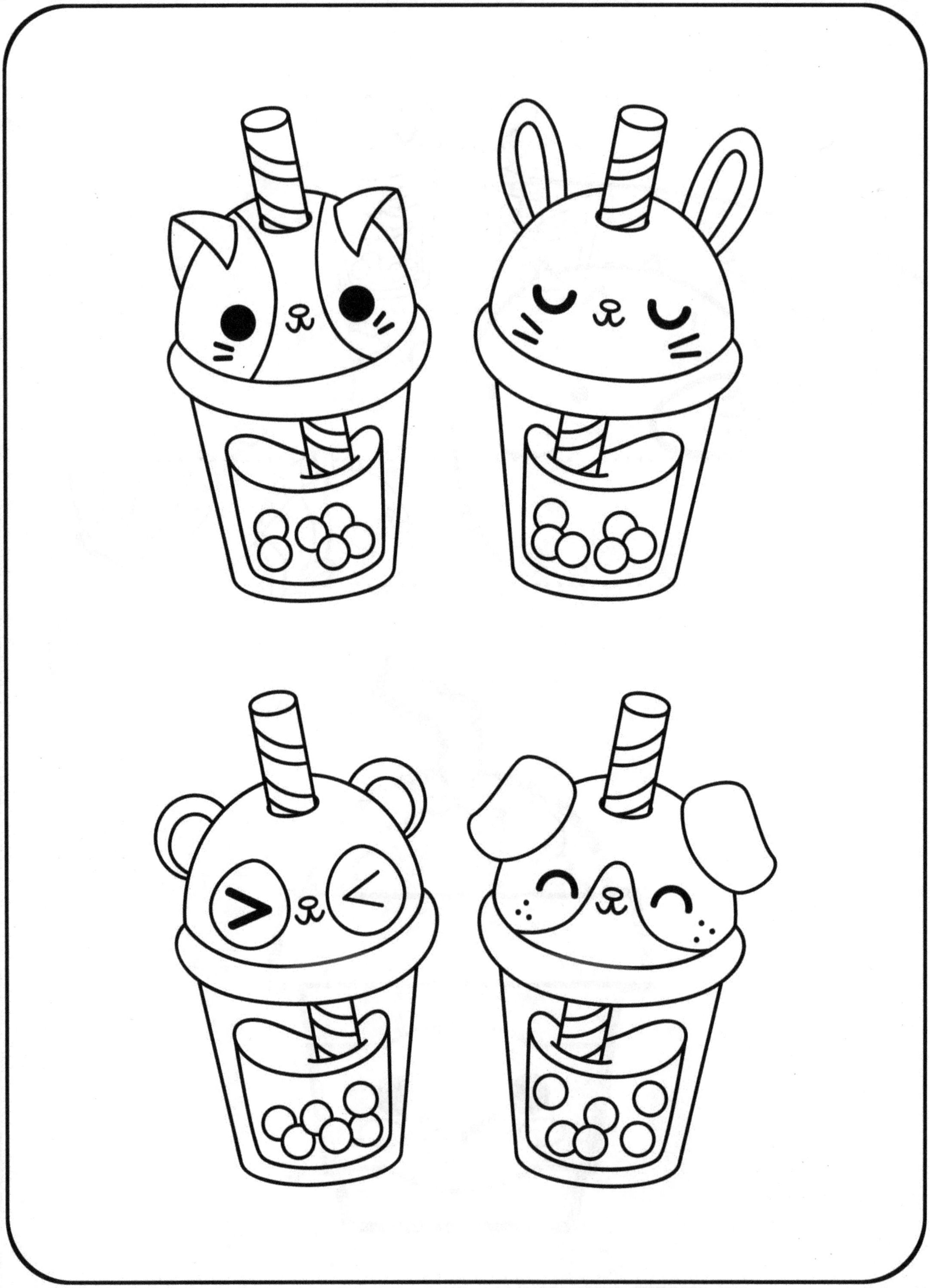

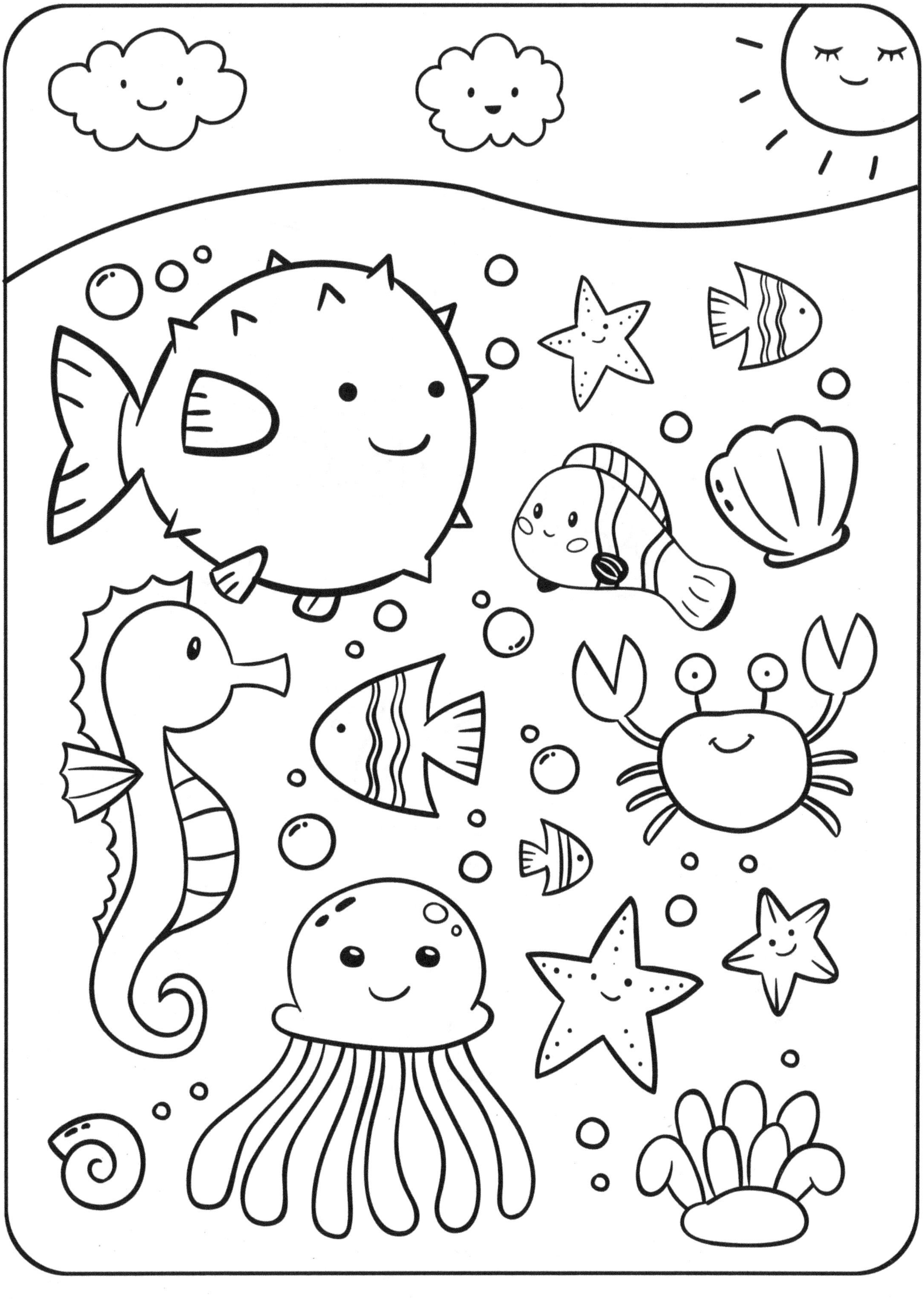

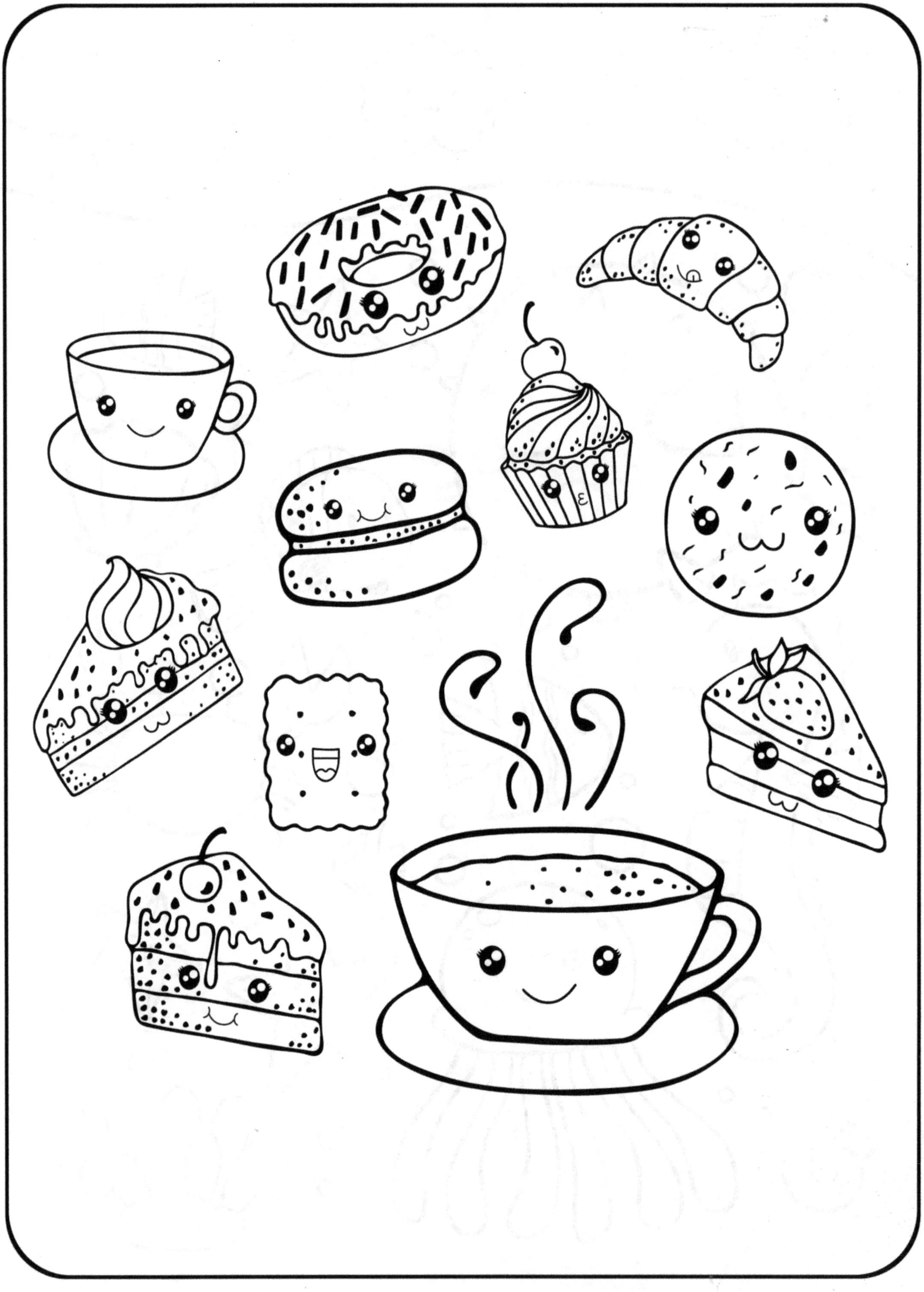

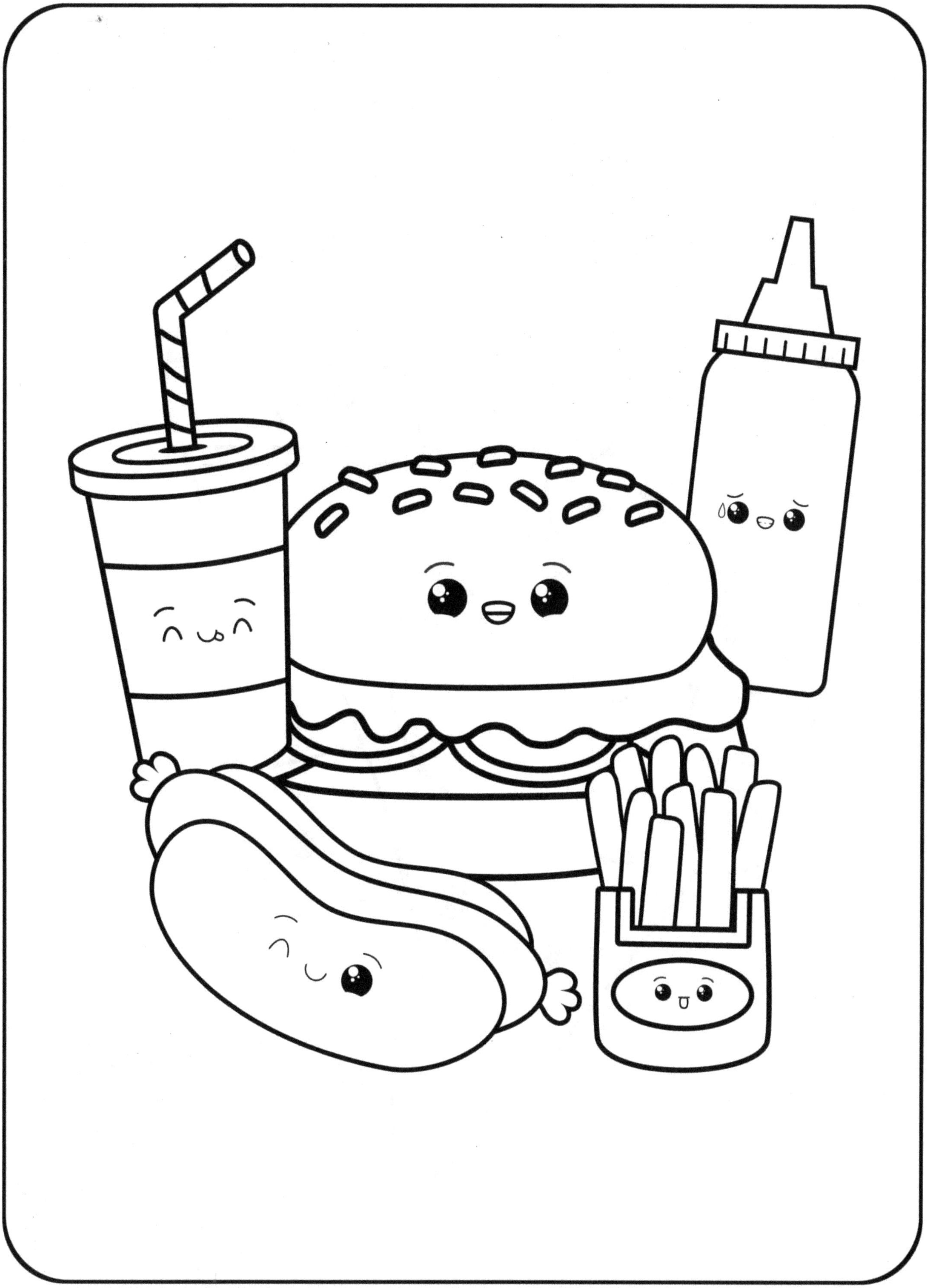

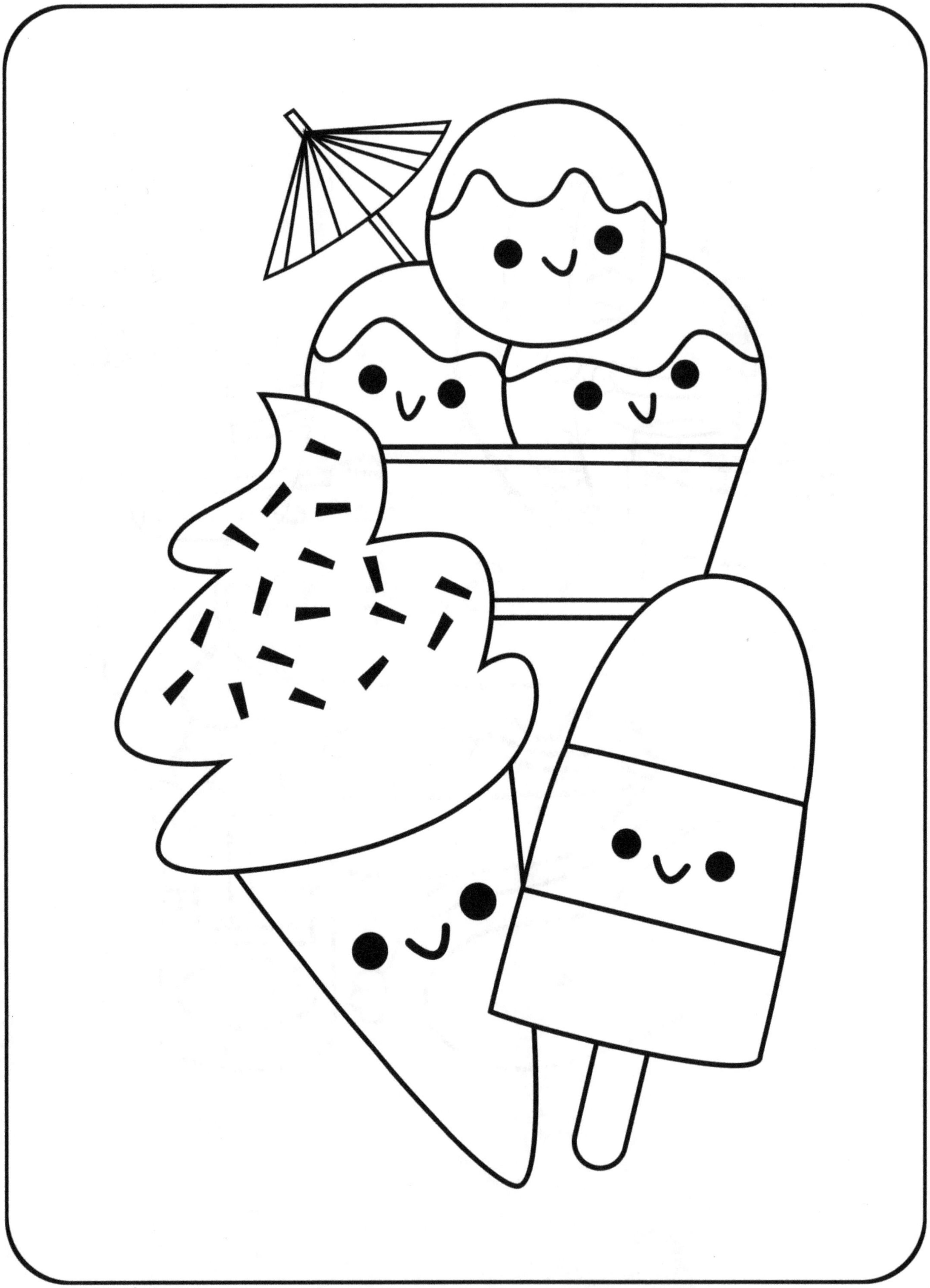

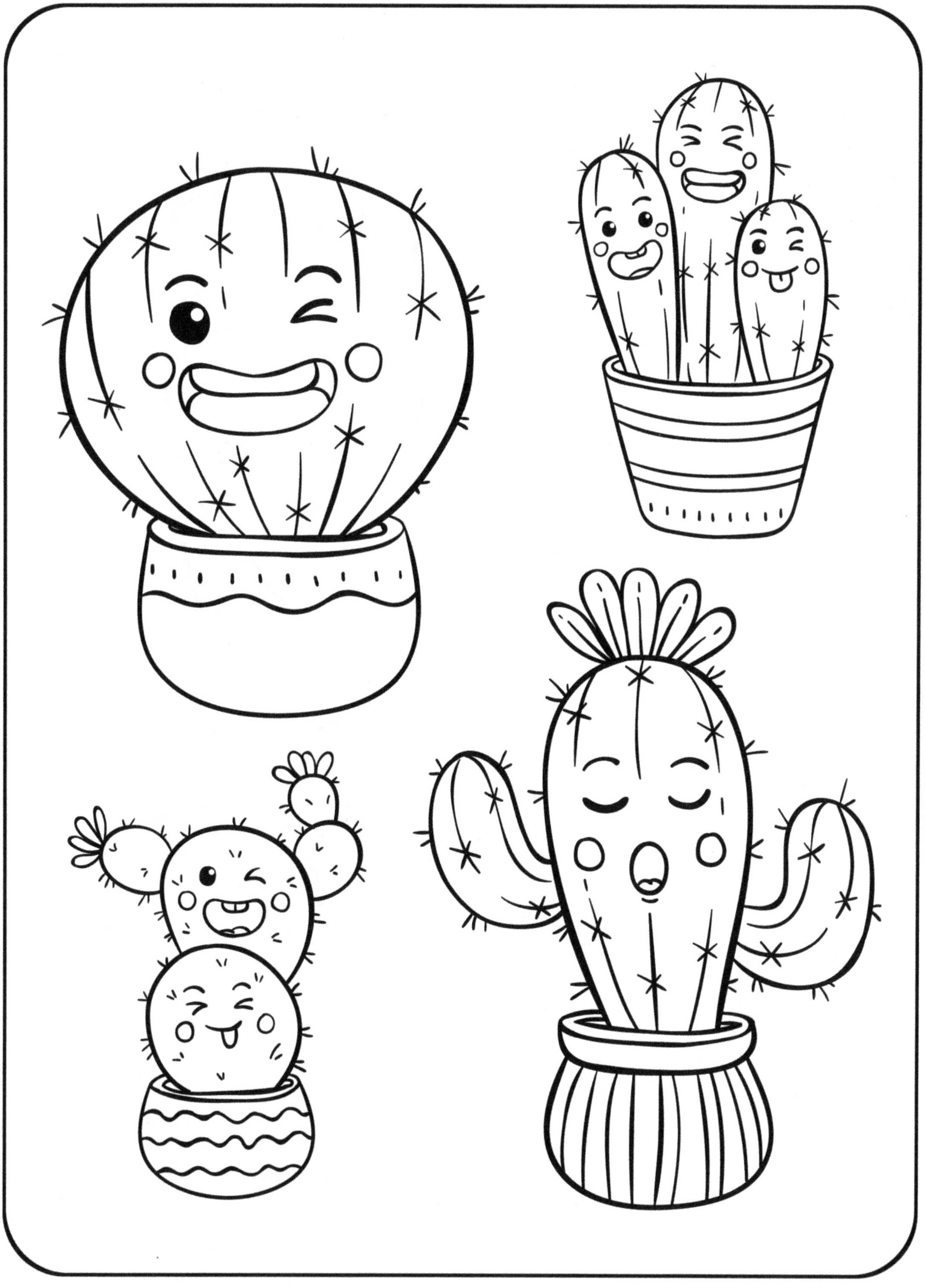

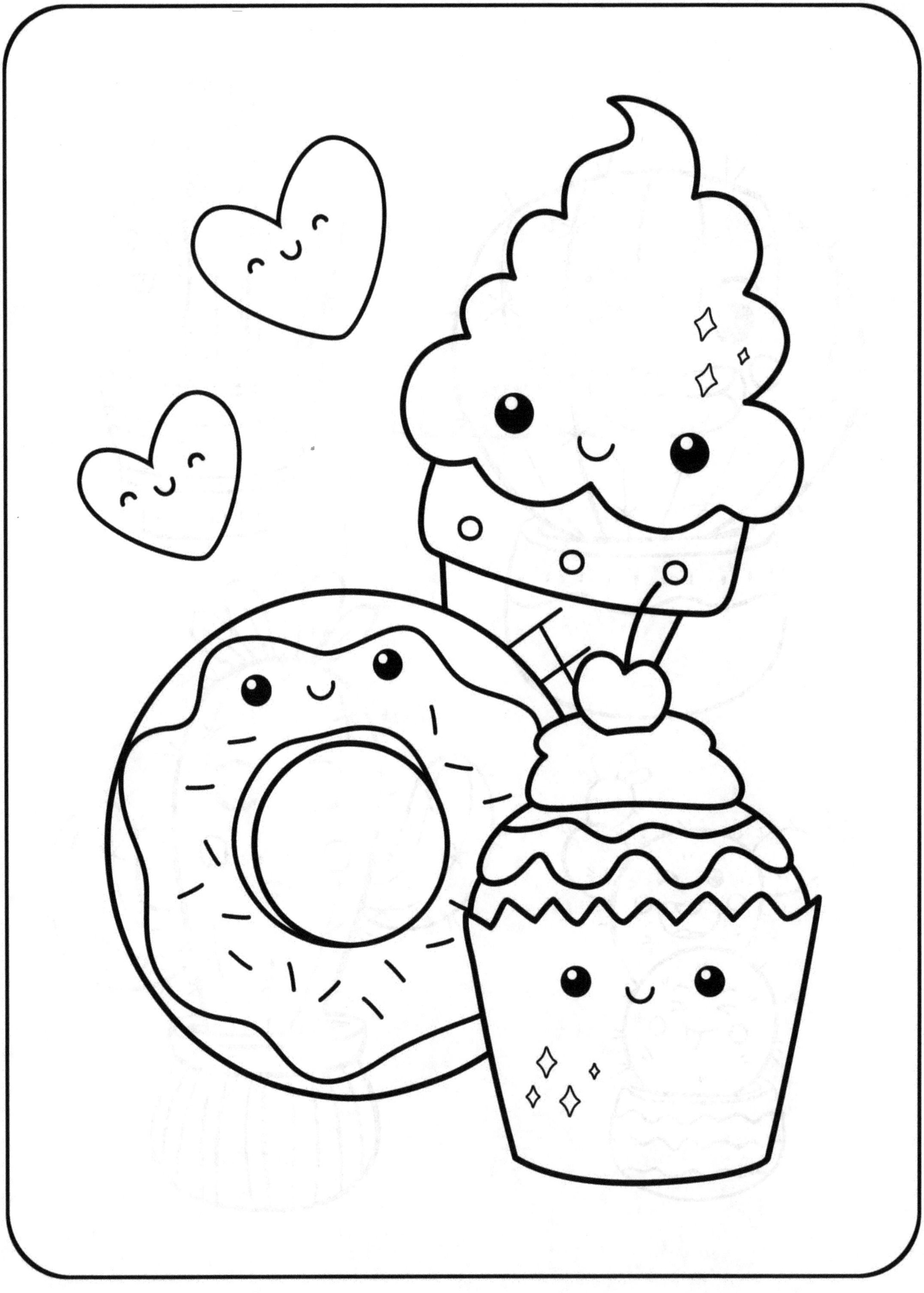

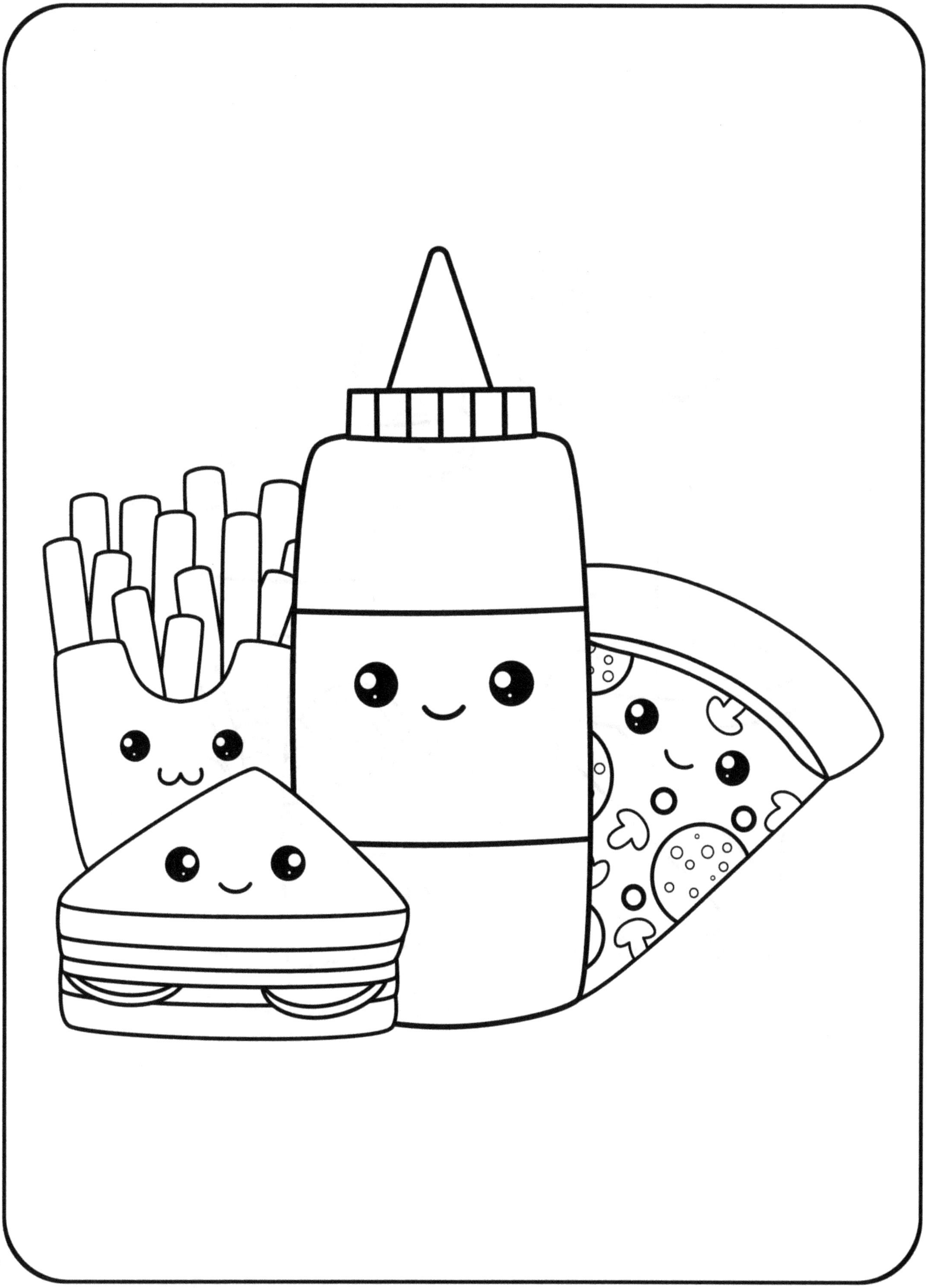

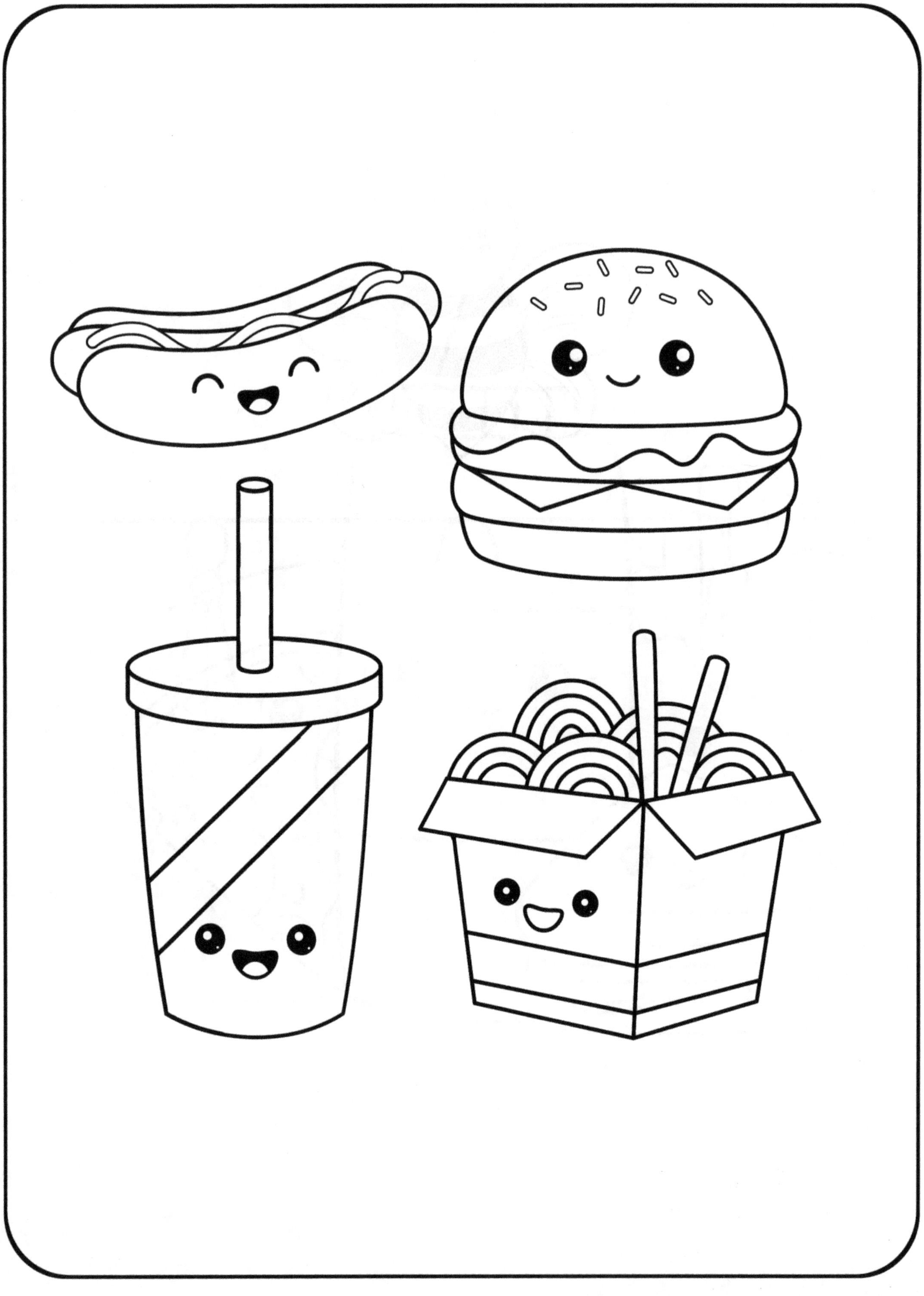

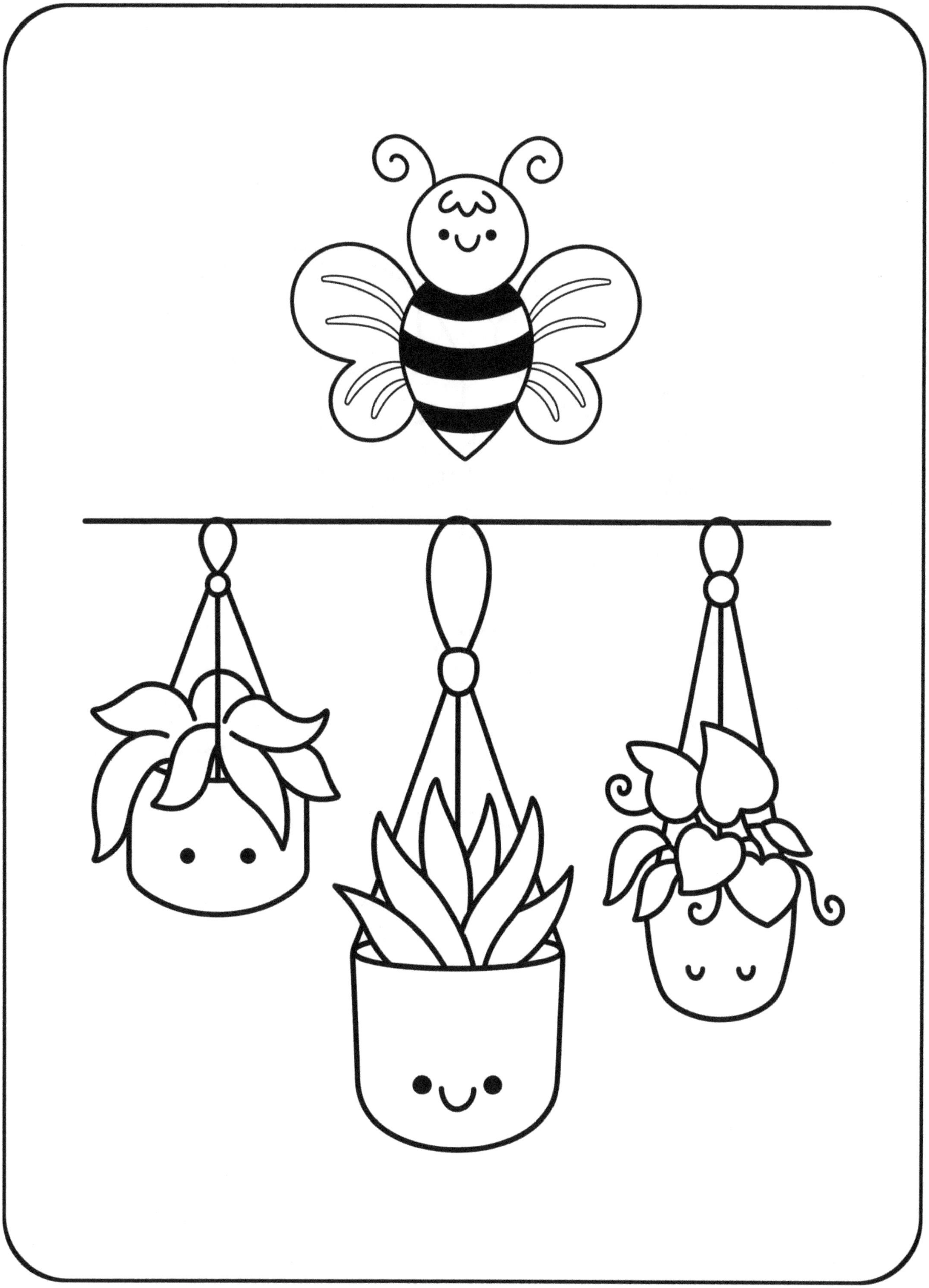

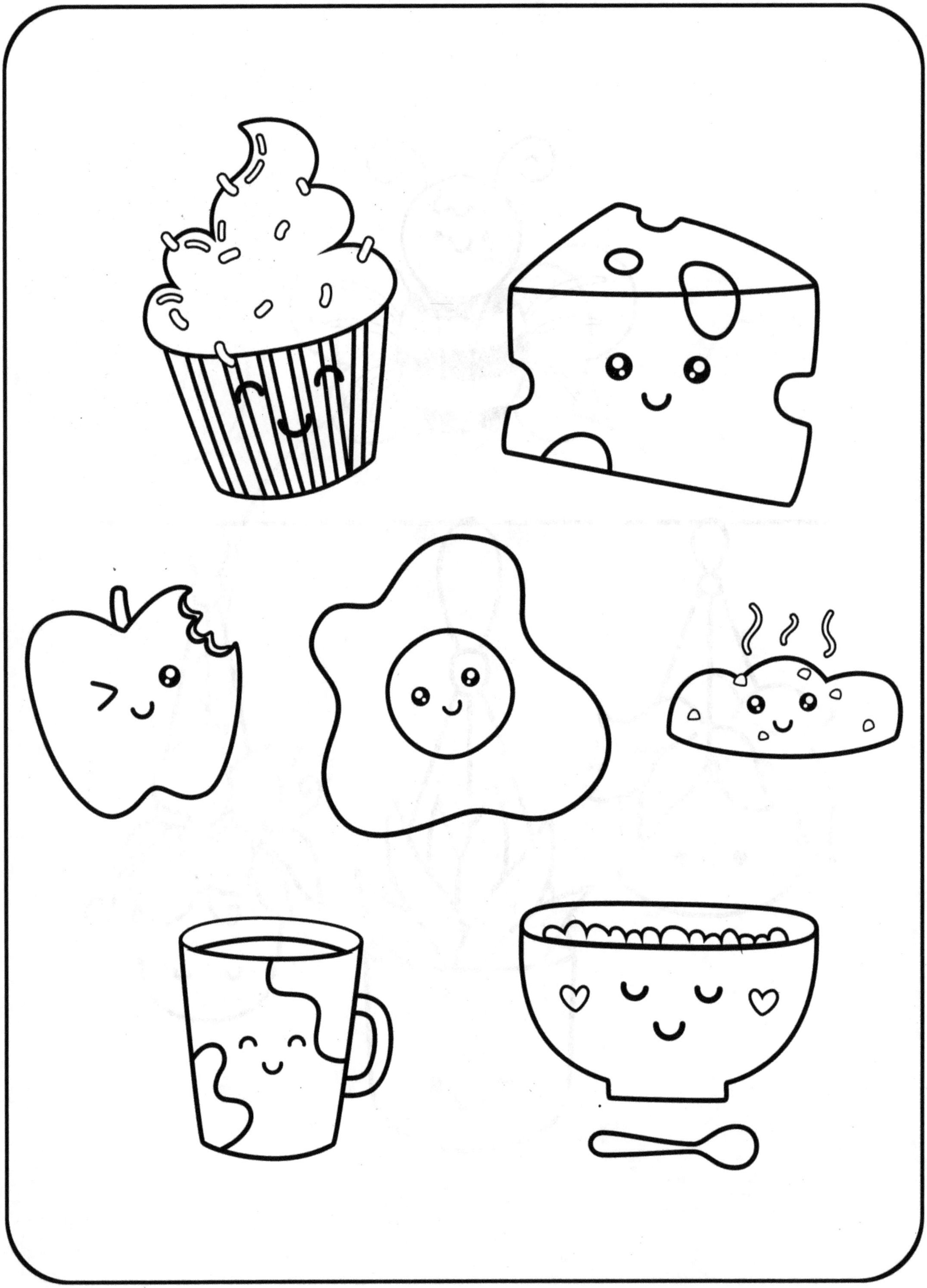

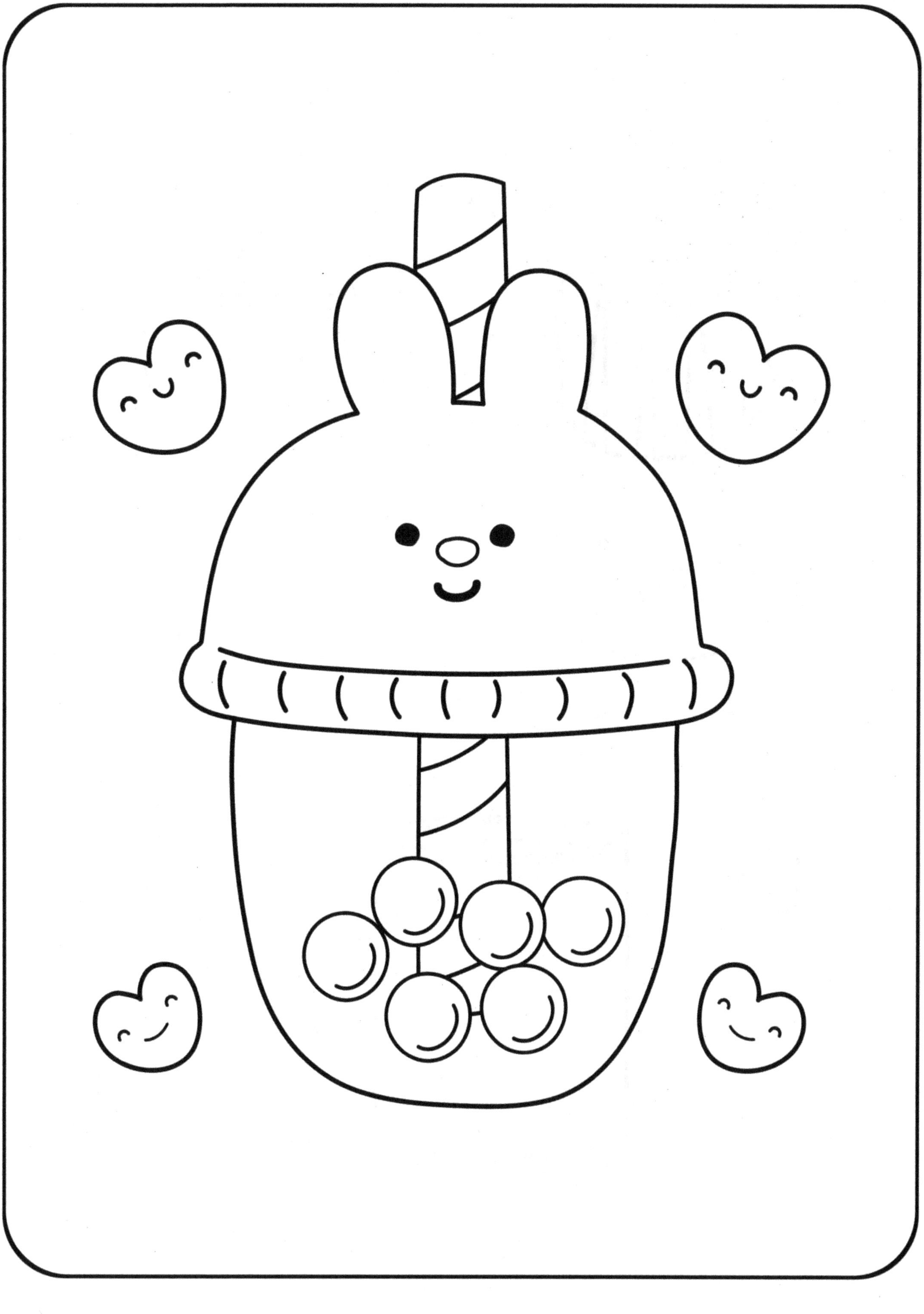

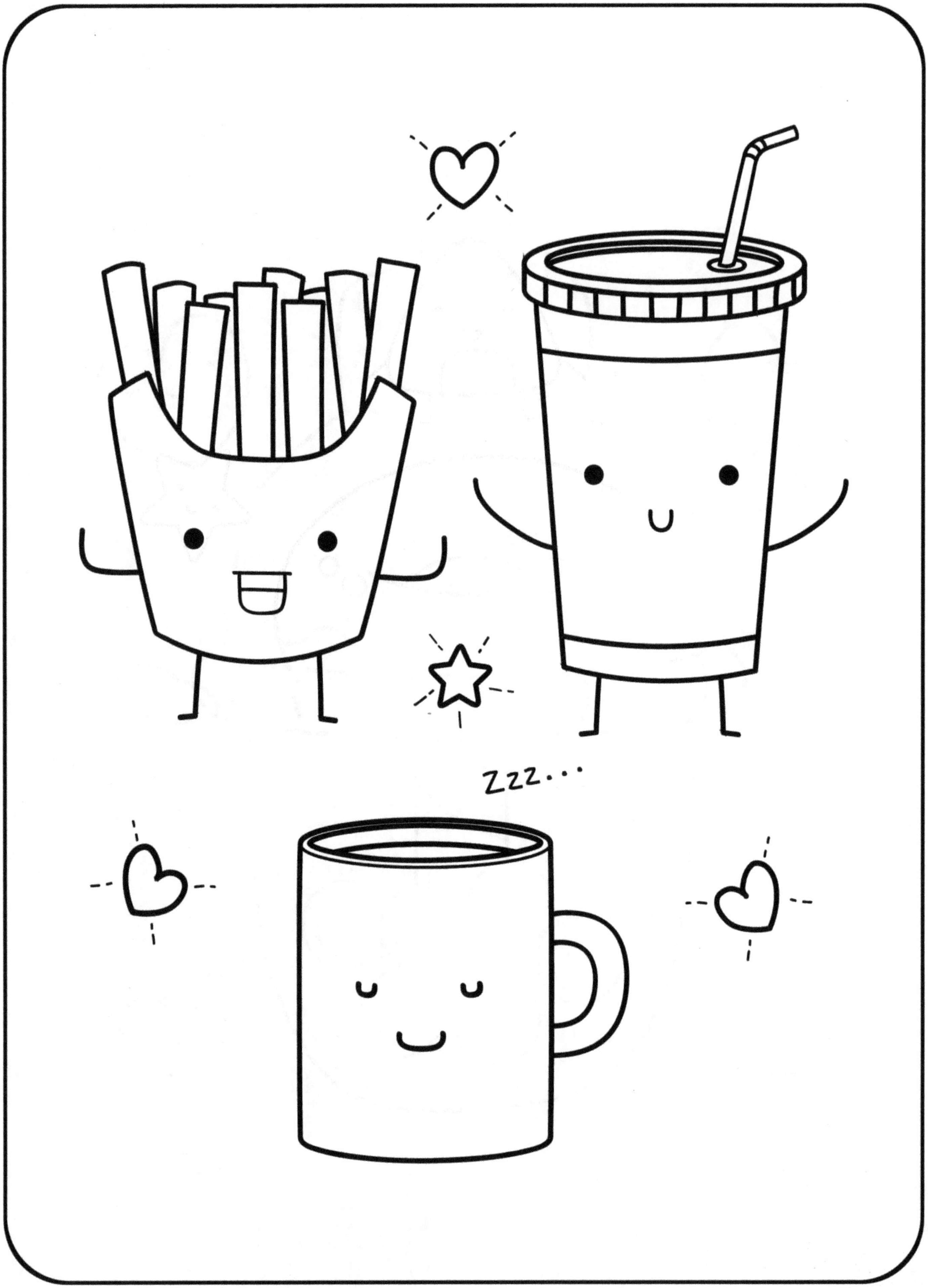
ZZZ...

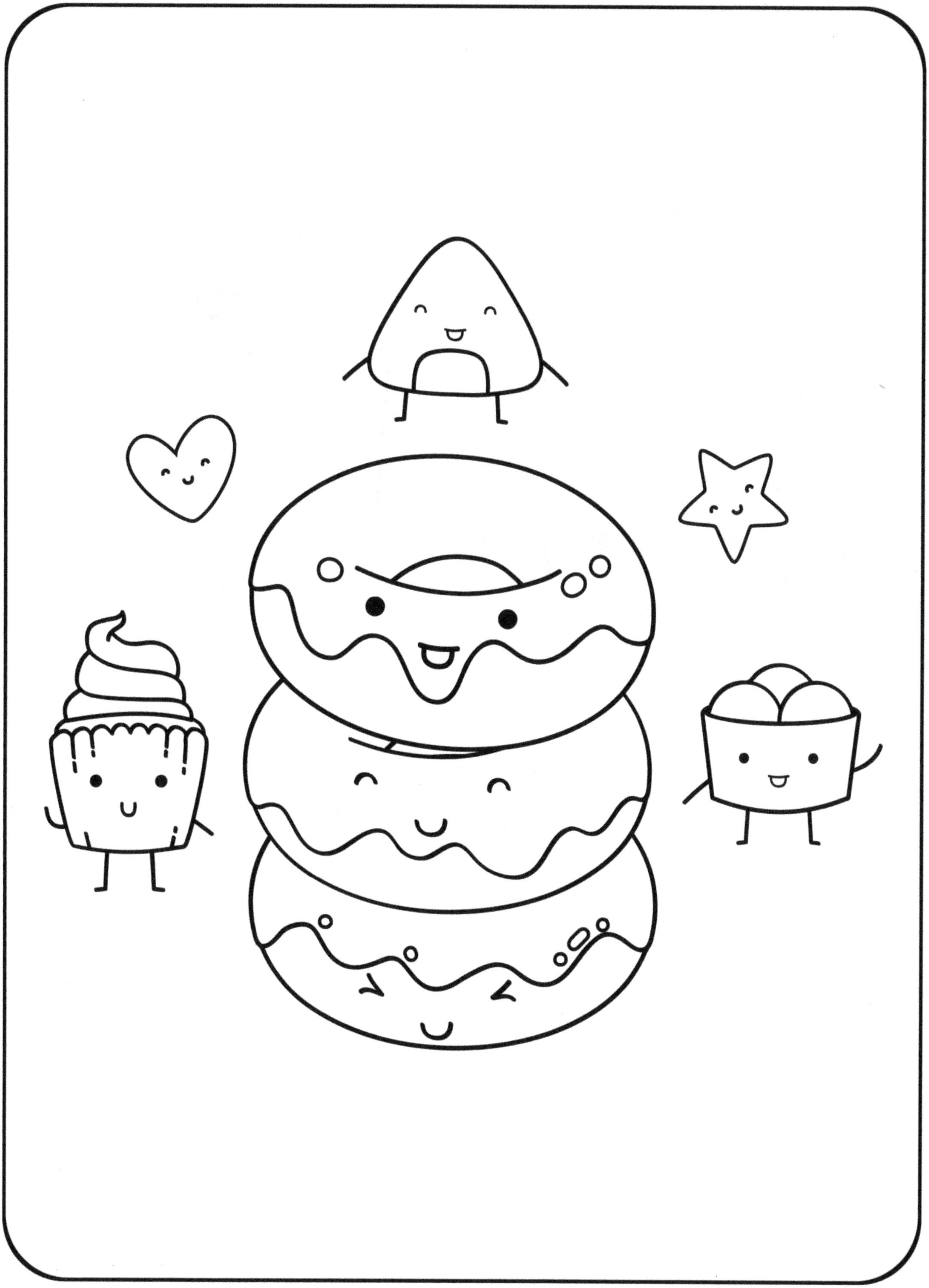

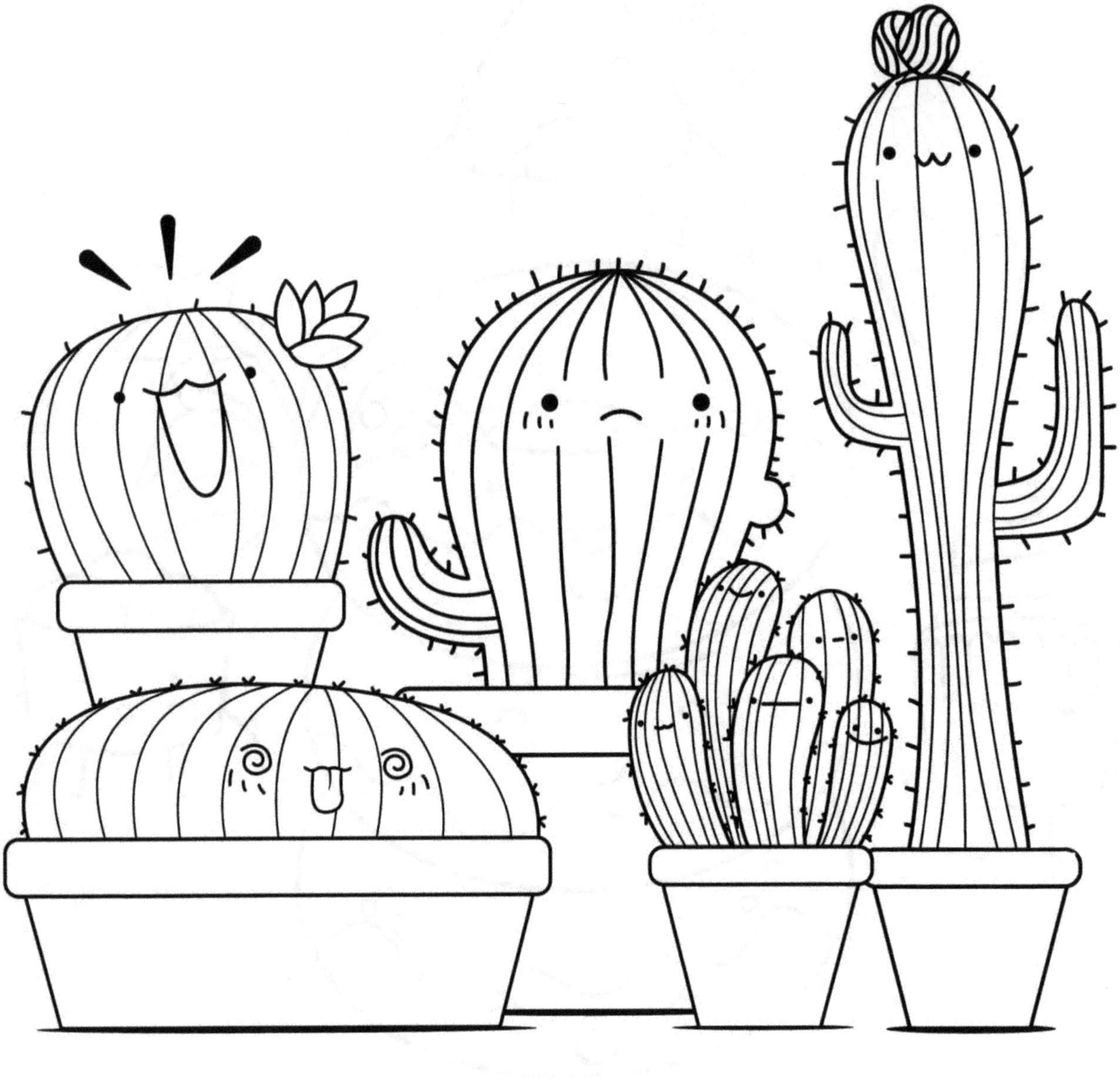

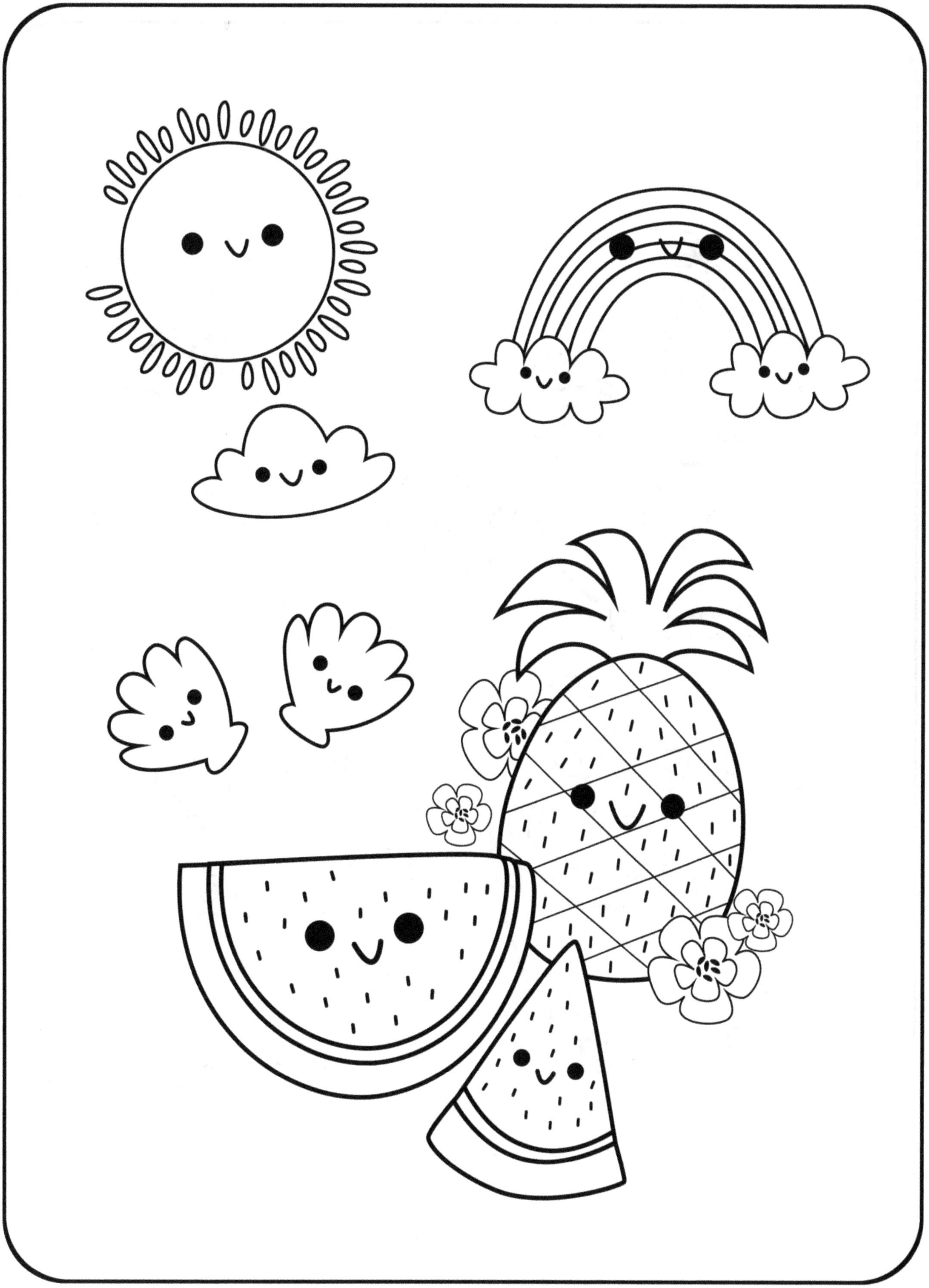

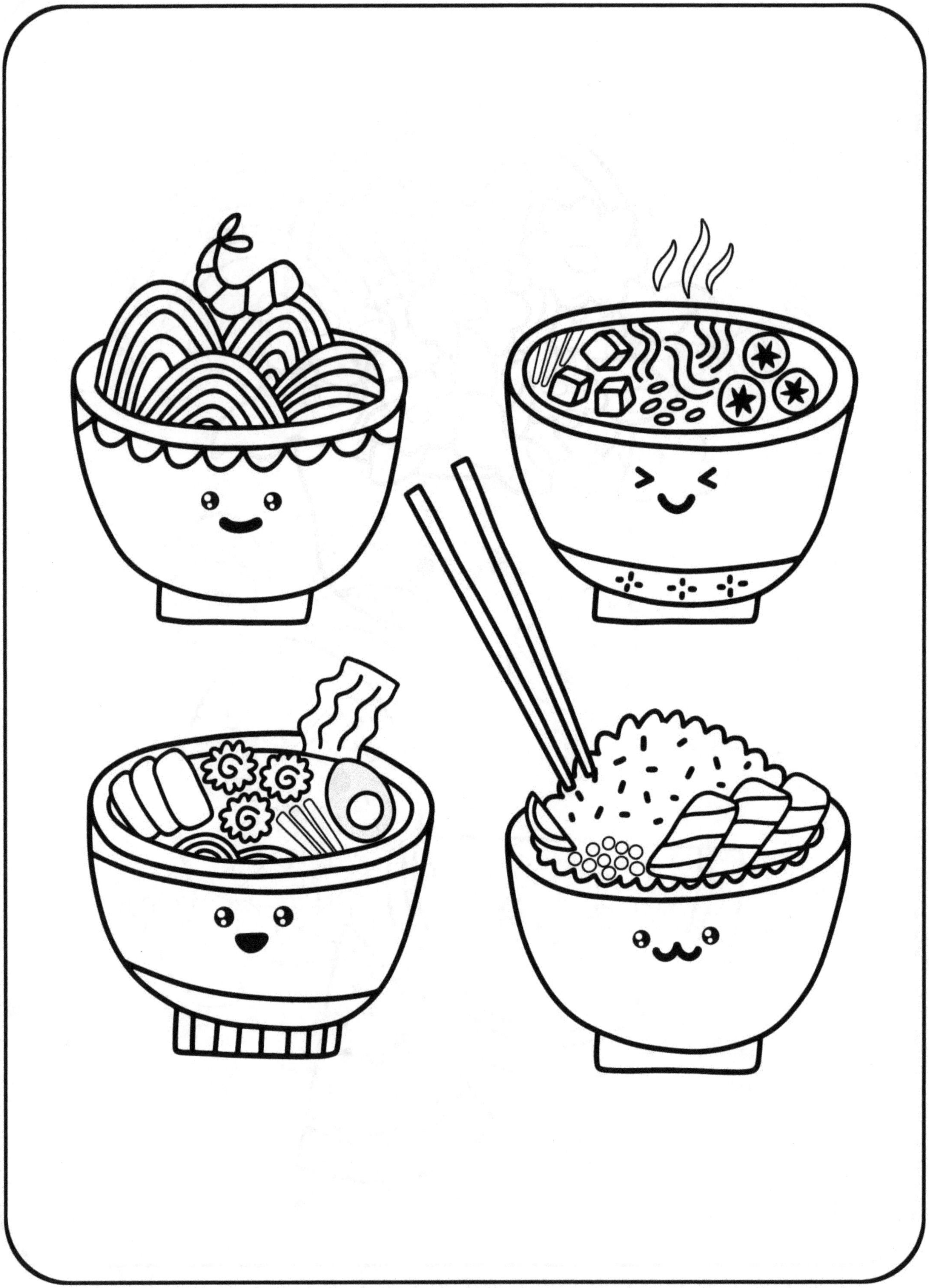

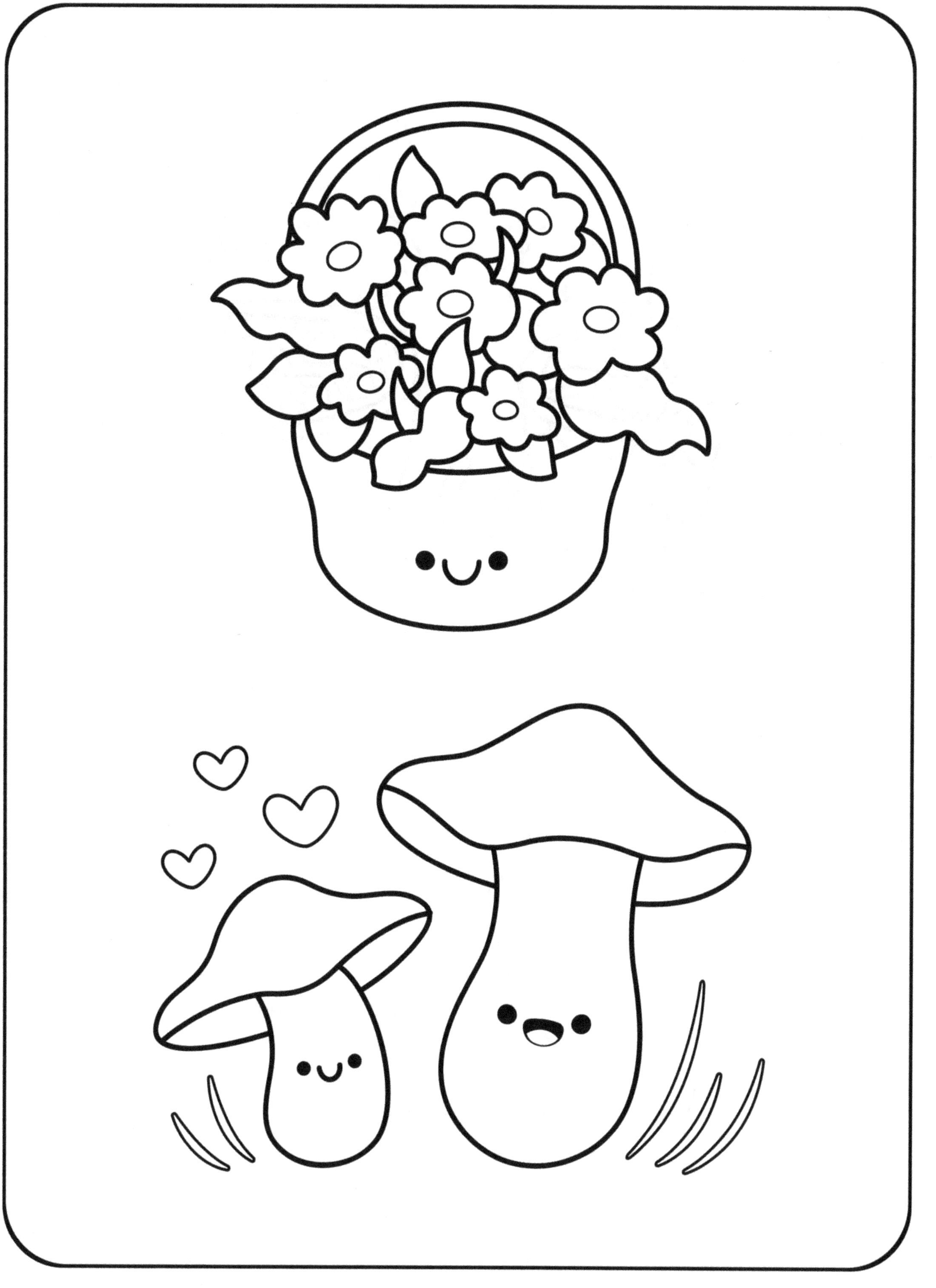

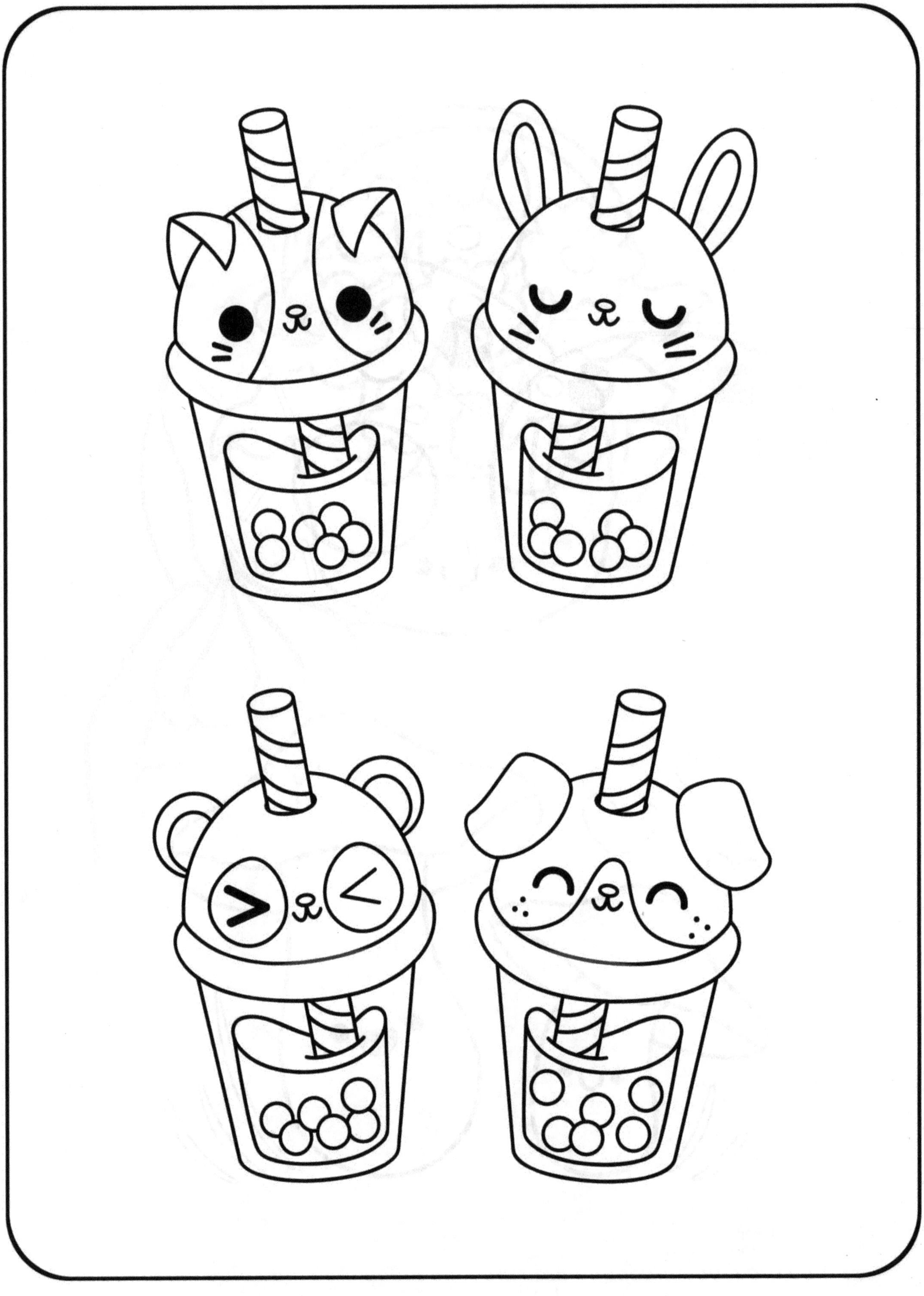

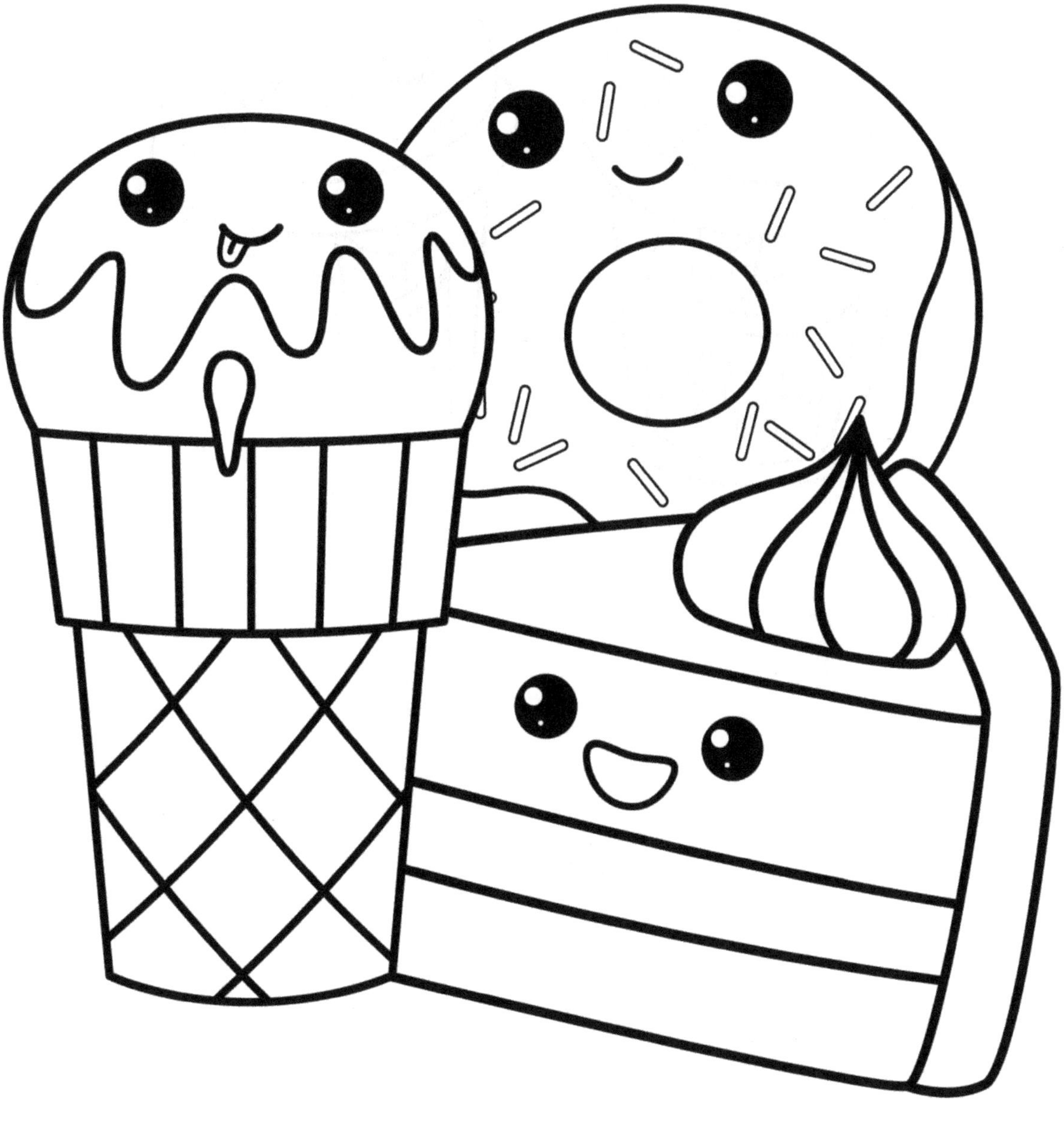

CPSIA information can be obtained
at www.ICGtesting.com
Printed in the USA
BVHW051753021221
623087BV00007B/310

9 788775 773169